TOP DOG

TOP DOG

thelwell's
COMPLETE CANINE
COMPENDIUM

MAGNUM BOOKS
Methuen Paperbacks Ltd

A Magnum Book

TOP DOG

0 413 34660 9

First published 1964 by Methuen and Co. Ltd
Methuen Paperbacks edition first published 1976
This (Magnum Books) reprint 1976

Copyright © 1962, 1963, 1964 by Norman Thelwell
and Beaverbrook Newspapers Ltd

Magnum Books are published by Methuen Paperbacks Ltd
11 New Fetter Lane, London EC4P 4EE

Made and printed in Great Britain
by Richard Clay (The Chaucer Press) Ltd
Bungay, Suffolk

Most of the drawings in this book
were taken from the *Sunday Express*

CONTENTS

CHOOSING YOUR DOG

THERE IS A RIGHT AND A WRONG TIME TO TAKE
A PUP FROM ITS MOTHER

TAKE GREAT PAINS WHEN CHOOSING.

NO TWO DOGS ARE EVER THE SAME

THEY ARE ALL IRRESISTIBLE WHEN VERY YOUNG . . .

BUT MAKE SURE YOU KNOW WHAT HE'LL LOOK LIKE
WHEN HE GROWS UP.

IT IS IMPORTANT TO PICK THE RIGHT BREED FOR
YOUR HOME...

THE WRONG CHOICE CAN BE EMBARRASSING . .

SOME TYPES ARE UNHAPPY.
IN MODERN FLATS . . . . .

OTHERS DON'T FIT THEIR
SURROUNDINGS.

DON'T HAVE A DOG THAT

TAKES OVER THE HOUSE . . . . .

SOME DOGS ARE OVER AFFECTIONATE . . . . .

.... BUT THEY'RE BETTER THAN THOSE THAT
DON'T CARE

CERTAIN CHARACTERISTICS CAN BE VERY
USEFUL IN THE HOME ....

BUT DOGS ARE NOT SUITED TO EVERY TASK

SO IF YOU WANT A WATCHDOG —

MAKE SURE YOU GET A GOOD ONE

BUT NEVER BUY ONE THAT'S **TOO** KEEN.

TRAINING

DOG LOVERS MUST BE PREPARED TO SPEND
CONSIDERABLE TIME HOUSE TRAINING A PUP

NEVER LET HIM SEE YOU GET RUFFLED . . .

MAKE SURE HE KNOWS
WHERE HIS SAND TRAY
IS KEPT . . . . .

AND KEEP AN EYE OPEN FOR SIGNS THAT
HE WANTS TO GO OUT.

YOUR FIRST TASK IS TO TEACH HIM TO SIT —

START BY GIVING THE COMMAND 'SIT'

REPEAT THE WORD CLEARLY WHILE PRESSING
FIRMLY DOWNWARD ON HIS HINDQUARTERS —

NEXT GIVE THE COMMAND
                    'COME HERE BOY' .....

... HE WILL THEN SIT.

NEXT YOU MUST TEACH HIM TO COME TO YOU —

FIRST TRY TO GET HIM TO GO AWAY

IF SUCCESSFUL, GIVE THE COMMAND 'COME'

THEN PRODUCE A PLATE OF LIVER AND
GRAVY......

AND DON'T FORGET TO PAT HIM FOR DOING AS
HE'S TOLD.

DOGS THAT JUMP UP CAN BE IRRITATING.....

HE MUST BE TAUGHT THE MEANING OF THE WORD
'DOWN'

DON'T BE DISCOURAGED BY FAILURES.....

HE WILL HAVE TO GET DOWN IN THE END.

TEACHING YOUR DOG TO DO TRICKS
IS NOT EASY.....

HE MAY EVEN SEEM STUPID AT FIRST

BUT JUST WHEN YOU FEEL THAT YOU WILL
NEVER GET THROUGH TO HIM.....

HE WILL SUDDENLY SURPRISE YOU

REMEMBER THAT DOGS
DO NOT UNDERSTAND COMPLICATED INSTRUCTIONS

SO KEEP ALL COMMANDS SIMPLE

USE A FIRM, DETERMINED VOICE

AND REPEAT AS OFTEN AS NECESSARY.

Food and Exercise

IT IS AS BAD TO OVERFEED AS TO UNDERFEED
YOUR DOG

RAW MEAT IS HIS NATURAL FOOD.....

....BUT HE CAN OFTEN BE TEMPTED BY FISH

POULTRY IS DANGEROUS FOR DOGS

IF HE BEGS AT TABLE — IGNORE HIM

AND DON'T GIVE HIM TOO MANY SWEETS

YOU WILL SOON GET TO KNOW
THE SORT OF THING THAT TEMPTS HIS PALATE —
BUT ABOVE ALL . . . .

DON'T ALLOW HIM TO PICK UP TIT-BITS
WHEN HE'S OUT.

CHOOSING THE RIGHT TINNED FOODS CAN BE
CONFUSING ...

THEY ARE ALL VERY CONVENIENT...

AND MOST OF THEM ARE DELICIOUS

BUT DOGS CAN BE DISCRIMINATING
EATERS . . . .

SO WHY NOT LET HIM MAKE HIS OWN CHOICE.

IF LEFT TO THEMSELVES, DOGS TEND
TO BE LAZY ...

REGULAR EXERCISE IS THEREFORE NECESSARY

TO KEEP THEM FIT

SOME REQUIRE VERY LITTLE ROOM FOR THIS . . . . .

.... OTHERS RATHER MORE .

HEALTH AND CLEANLINESS

THE GENERAL CONDITION OF YOUR DOG SHOULD

BE CHECKED DAILY

SEE THAT HIS TEETH ARE CLEAN AND WHITE

AND HIS NOSE COLD AND DAMP

TEST HIS HEARING —

ENSURE THAT HIS EYES ARE BRIGHT
AND CLEAR ...

THAT HIS FEET ARE
SCRUPULOUSLY
CLEAN ...

AND THAT HIS TOE NAILS ARE NOT TOO LONG

GROOMING SHOULD START WHILST HE IS A SMALL PUPPY

MAKE A GAME OF IT AND HE WILL GROW TO ENJOY IT

VIGOROUS BRUSHING WILL BE NECESSARY
TO REMOVE HIS LOOSE HAIRS

IF YOU SUSPECT THAT HE
HAS PICKED UP FLEAS . . .

SPRINKLE HIM LIBERALLY WITH
A GOOD DUSTING POWDER

58

RUB WELL INTO THE COAT

THEY WILL NOT STAY
ON HIM FOR LONG

IT WILL SOMETIMES BE NECESSARY

TO BATHE YOUR DOG

GETTING HIM INTO THE WATER ...

.. MAY BE A LITTLE TEDIOUS ...

BUT HE WILL CERTAINLY LOOK BETTER
FOR THE EFFORT.

DOGS IN THE HOME

YOUR DOG SHOULD NOT BE ALLOWED

TO MONOPOLISE THE BEST CHAIR

TRY TO EJECT HIM WITHOUT FUSS

NEVER RESORT TO VIOLENCE ...

IT IS CHEAPER TO BUY A NEW CHAIR.

A COMFORTABLE PLACE TO SLEEP IS, HOWEVER,
ESSENTIAL TO YOUR PET'S WELLBEING

A RAISED CANVAS COUCH WILL KEEP HIM
OUT OF DRAUGHTS

AND WICKER
BASKETS ARE
ALWAYS
POPULAR

YOU WILL SOON DISCOVER THE SORT OF BED
HE PREFERS.

WISE DOG OWNERS WILL ALSO CONSTRUCT...

. A STRONG WATERPROOF KENNEL ...

... TO PROVIDE EMERGENCY SHELTER ...

... IN BAD WEATHER.

YOU SHOULD ENSURE THAT YOUR GARDEN FENCE
IS DOG PROOF

YOUR NEIGHBOUR MAY NOT

WELCOME YOUR PET

You CERTAINLY WON'T WELCOME HIS

DOGS OUT OF DOORS

WHEN ON THE STREET YOUR DOG MUST BE KEPT
UNDER STRICT CONTROL

TEACH HIM TO WALK QUIETLY TO 'HEEL' ...

MAKE SURE HE IS FIRMLY RESTRICTED

BY THE LEAD....

...AND SEE THAT HE LEARNS ALL ABOUT
MODERN TRAFFIC

MEETING OTHER DOGS CAN BE TRICKY

RESTRAIN YOUR OWN ANIMAL ...

... AND KEEP CALM ...

ABOVE ALL ... AVOID A FIGHT

IT IS WORTH REMEMBERING THAT THERE ARE
FEW MORE USEFUL COMPANIONS ON THE BEACH
THAN A DOG

FOR PROVIDING PRIVACY....

... GUARDING YOUR CLOTHES ...

AND BRINGING THINGS TO YOU.

DOGS AND THE LAW

OWNERS MUST BE PREPARED TO ACCEPT FULL
RESPONSIBILITY FOR THEIR DOGS' BEHAVIOUR

NO ANIMAL IS ENTITLED TO ATTACK A PERSON
ENGAGED IN LAWFUL PURSUITS . . . .

IT IS AN OFFENCE TO LET HIM OUT
WITHOUT A COLLAR

OR TO ALLOW HIM TO 'LOITER'
ON THE STREETS

HE MUST NOT BE PERMITTED TO DRAW A CART,
CARRIAGE OR BARROW ON THE
QUEEN'S HIGHWAY

AND ALL ROAD ACCIDENTS IN WHICH HE IS INVOLVED
MUST BE REPORTED

UNDER NO CIRCUMSTANCES MUST HE INTERFERE
WITH FARM ANIMALS

AND HE MUST BE KEPT
ON A LEAD IN PUBLIC
PARKS

IT IS ILLEGAL TO TREAT HIM UNLESS YOU ARE
A QUALIFIED VET

OR TO ALLOW HIM TO BOARD A BUS

UNACCOMPANIED

AND NEEDLESS TO SAY . . . .

IT IS A SERIOUS OFFENCE TO ILLTREAT HIM
IN ANY WAY WHATSOEVER.

MAN'S BEST FRIEND

THE GUN DOG

THE LAP DOG

THE SHEEP DOG

THE HUNTING DOG

THE GUARD DOG

THE RACING DOG

THE RESCUE DOG

THE MESSENGER DOG

THE TRACKER DOG

THE TOY DOG

THE WAR DOG

THE GUIDE DOG

THE SHOW DOG

THE POLICE DOG

THE DRAUGHT DOG

THE STRAY DOG

USEFUL TIPS

WHEN DEALING WITH DOGS, IT IS AS WELL

TO REMEMBER . . . .

HOW QUICKLY THEIR ATTENTION

MAY BE DIVERTED...

...FROM ONE SUBJECT...

... TO ANOTHER

SOME DOGS BARK AND BARK AND BARK . . . .

...UNTIL THE SOUND BECOMES
UNBEARABLE ...

THE ONLY WAY TO STOP A DOG FROM
BARKING...

... IS TO LEARN THE VIOLIN .

THE DETERMINATION OF THE AVERAGE

DOG ....

... TO BE WITH HIS BELOVED MASTER ...

... AT ALL TIMES ...

... IS ASTONISHING

A DOG'S NOSE IS A
HIGHLY SENSITIVE ORGAN ...

ENABLING HIM TO TRACK DOWN FOR MAN,
WITH SPEED AND ACCURACY...

. ALL MANNER OF OBJECTS...

... WHICH MIGHT OTHERWISE BE LOST.

MOST DOGS LOVE TO TRAVEL IN CARS . . .

...SOME PREFER TO TRAVEL HALF IN - HALF OUT

THEY CAN BE A NUISANCE AT TIMES ...

...BUT THEY CERTAINLY HAVE THEIR USES

FINALLY REMEMBER THAT DOGS ARE NOBLE,
COURAGEOUS CREATURES

AND CAN STRIKE TERROR
INTO THE HEART OF AN
ENEMY

THEY WILL ATTACK FEARLESSLY

WHEN DANGER THREATENS . . .

BUT ARE GENTLE AND AFFECTIONATE
WITH PEOPLE THEY LIKE